I0448696

Congressional
Research
Service

Clean Air Issues in the 113th Congress: An Overview

James E. McCarthy
Specialist in Environmental Policy

November 4, 2013

Congressional Research Service

7-5700

www.crs.gov

R42895

Summary

As the 113th Congress continues consideration of air quality issues, oversight of Environmental Protection Agency (EPA) regulatory actions is expected to remain the main focus. Of particular interest are EPA's Clean Air Act regulations on emissions of greenhouse gases. President Obama's June 25 announcement of initiatives to address climate change and EPA's subsequent (September 20) proposal of GHG emission standards for new fossil-fueled power plants sparked renewed interest in the issue.

Air quality has improved substantially in the United States in the 40 years of EPA's Clean Air Act (CAA) regulation. According to the agency's science advisers and others, however, more needs to be done to protect public health and the environment from the effects of air pollution. Thus, the agency continues to promulgate regulations using authority given it by Congress in CAA amendments more than 20 years ago. Members of Congress from both parties have raised questions about the cost-effectiveness of some of these regulations and/or whether the agency has exceeded statutory authority in promulgating them. Others in Congress have supported EPA, noting that the Clean Air Act, often affirmed in court decisions, has authorized or required the agency's actions.

EPA's regulatory actions on GHG emissions have been the main focus of congressional interest in 2013. Although the Obama Administration has consistently said it would prefer that Congress pass new legislation to address climate change, such legislation now appears unlikely. Instead, over the last four years, EPA has developed GHG emission standards using its existing CAA authority. Relying on a finding that GHGs endanger public health and welfare, the agency promulgated GHG emission standards for cars and light trucks on May 7, 2010, and again on October 15, 2012, and for larger trucks on September 15, 2011. The implementation of these standards, in turn, triggered permitting and Best Available Control Technology requirements for new major stationary sources of GHGs (power plants, manufacturing facilities, etc.).

It is the triggering of standards and permit requirements for stationary sources that has raised the most concern in Congress. A proposal to limit carbon dioxide emissions from new power plants is the focus of attention currently, but other sources (refineries, cement plants, etc.) could be subject to GHG emission controls under the same statutory authority. In addition to the proposed standards for new power plants, the President has directed EPA to develop standards for *existing* power plants by June 2015. Legislation has been introduced in both the House and Senate aimed at preventing EPA from implementing such requirements. The House passed several of these bills in the 112th Congress, but none passed the Senate. Meanwhile, EPA has implemented permit and Best Available Control Technology requirements for new stationary sources of GHGs. A challenge to these requirements will be heard by the Supreme Court in early 2014.

Besides addressing climate change, EPA has taken action on a number of other air pollution regulations, generally in response to court actions remanding previous rules. Remanded rules included the Clean Air Interstate Rule (CAIR) and Clean Air Mercury Rule—rules designed to control the long-range transport of sulfur dioxide, nitrogen oxides, and mercury from power plants through cap-and-trade programs. Other remanded rules included hazardous air pollutant standards for boilers and cement kilns. EPA also recently proposed a controversial rule to lower the sulfur content of gasoline, in conjunction with tighter ("Tier3") standards for motor vehicle emissions.

EPA is also reviewing ambient air quality standards (NAAQS) for ozone and other widespread air pollutants. An ozone NAAQS proposal is expected in 2014. NAAQS serve as EPA's definition of clean air, and drive a range of regulatory controls. EPA's review process for the NAAQS, mandated at five-year intervals by the Clean Air Act, has also faced opposition in Congress.

Contents

Figures

Contacts

Introduction

With the 113ᵗʰ Congress divided like the 112ᵗʰ into a Republican-controlled House and a majority-Democratic Senate, and the President having been re-elected, environmental issues, including those related to air quality, reflect those of the last Congress. In that period, congressional interest in air quality issues was dominated by efforts to prevent the Environmental Protection Agency (EPA) from promulgating and implementing new emission control requirements. Often under court order, EPA has used authorities Congress gave it in the Clean Air Act amendments of 1970, 1977, and 1990 to address longstanding issues posed by emissions from various sources. EPA's regulations on greenhouse gas emissions from both mobile and stationary sources and on conventional and hazardous air pollutants emitted by electric power plants, cement kilns, and boilers have been of particular interest, as have the agency's efforts to revise ambient air quality standards for ozone and particulate matter. These issues remain in the 113ᵗʰ Congress; particularly in the House, efforts to restrain agency regulatory actions occupy a prominent place.

Both the House and Senate may also consider broader legislation designed to address regulation in general—bills such as the REINS Act (H.R. 367/S. 15), which would require congressional approval before regulations classified as major rules could take effect. If enacted, such legislation would affect new rules under the Clean Air Act as well as other statutes, but given the broad nature of the bills' purpose, they are not discussed here. For information on the REINS Act, see CRS Report R41651, *REINS Act: Number and Types of "Major Rules" in Recent Years*, by Maeve P. Carey and Curtis W. Copeland.

EPA's Greenhouse Gas Regulations

A continuing focus of congressional interest under the Clean Air Act (CAA) has been EPA regulatory actions to limit greenhouse gas (GHG) emissions using existing CAA authority. EPA actions have focused on six gases or groups of gases that multiple scientific studies have linked to climate change.[1] Of the six gases, carbon dioxide (CO_2), produced by combustion of fossil fuels, is by far the most prevalent, accounting for nearly 85% of annual emissions of the combined group when measured as CO_2 equivalents.

Members from both sides of the aisle, including a majority of the House in the 112ᵗʰ Congress, have expressed concerns about EPA proceeding with GHG regulations that could have major economic impacts. Some argue that the case for GHG controls has not been proven. Others maintain that EPA should delay taking such action until Congress more explicitly authorizes it.

EPA, by contrast, concludes that the Clean Air Act already requires action: a 2007 Supreme Court decision interpreting EPA's Clean Air Act authority, *Massachusetts v. EPA*,[2] found that the agency must weigh whether GHG emissions from new motor vehicles endanger public health and welfare and, if it concludes that they do, proceed with regulation of such vehicles. The agency made this endangerment finding in December 2009,[3] and proceeded to promulgate GHG emission

---

[1] The six are carbon dioxide (CO_2), methane (CH_4), nitrous oxide (N_2O), sulfur hexafluoride (SF_6), hydrofluorocarbons (HFCs), and perfluorocarbons (PFCs).

[2] 549 U.S. 497 (2007).

[3] 74 *Federal Register* 66496. While generally referred to as the "endangerment finding" (singular), the *Federal* (continued...)

standards for new 2012-2016 cars and light trucks, May 7, 2010.[4] (For information on these regulations, see CRS Report R40506, *Cars, Trucks, and Climate: EPA Regulation of Greenhouse Gases from Mobile Sources*, and CRS Report R41212, *EPA Regulation of Greenhouse Gases: Congressional Responses and Options*.)

The prospect of GHG standards for motor vehicles has not been particularly controversial. In May 2009, President Obama reached agreement with major U.S. and foreign auto manufacturers and other stakeholders regarding the substance of GHG emission and related fuel economy standards.[5] The auto industry supported a national agreement, in part, to avoid having to meet standards on a state-by-state basis; thus, it has not supported efforts to block EPA's motor vehicle GHG standards. A second round of standards, promulgated in October 2012,[6] was also preceded by an agreement with the auto industry and key stakeholders. (For additional details, see CRS Report R42721, *Automobile and Truck Fuel Economy (CAFE) and Greenhouse Gas Standards*.)

EPA and the National Highway Traffic Safety Administration (NHTSA) have also promulgated joint GHG emission and fuel economy standards for medium- and heavy-duty trucks,[7] which have been supported by the affected industries. (For a brief summary of these, see CRS Report R41563, *Clean Air Issues in the 112th Congress*.)

The decisions to move forward on GHG standards for new motor vehicles were seen by many, including EPA, as precedents for other potential standards. On December 23, 2010, the agency announced that it had reached a settlement agreement with 11 states, the City of New York, the District of Columbia, and 3 environmental groups under which it would propose GHG emission standards for power plants by July 26, 2011, and for refineries by December 10, 2011, with promulgation by May 2012 and November 2012 respectively. Power plants are the largest source of U.S. GHG emissions, accounting for one-third of the U.S. total, and petroleum refineries are the second largest industrial source of GHG emissions.

EPA has not fulfilled the terms of the two consent agreements. The agency has proposed the standards for new power plants, but other than that, has not yet taken the agreed-upon actions.

(...continued)

Register notice consists of two separate findings: a Finding That Greenhouse Gases Endanger Public Health and Welfare, and a Finding That Emissions of Greenhouse Gases from CAA Section 202(a) Sources Cause or Contribute to the Endangerment of Public Health and Welfare. [CAA Section 202(a) sources are new motor vehicles or new motor vehicle engines.]

[4] 75 *Federal Register* 25324. For additional information, including a link to the standards, see http://www.epa.gov/otaq/ climate/regulations htm#finalR. The agency subsequently (on October 15, 2012) promulgated GHG standards for model years 2017-2025.

[5] GHG emissions and fuel economy are directly related, because 94% of GHG emissions from light duty vehicles are the result of fuel combustion. The less fuel a vehicle uses, the lower will be its GHG emissions.

The President's announcement and related documents, including a Notice of Upcoming Joint Rulemaking to Establish Vehicle GHG Emissions and CAFE Standards, which appeared in the May 22, 2009, *Federal Register*, and both the draft and final emission standards can be found at http://www.epa.gov/otaq/climate/regulations.htm. For additional information, see CRS Report R42721, *Automobile and Truck Fuel Economy (CAFE) and Greenhouse Gas Standards*, by Brent D. Yacobucci, Bill Canis, and Richard K. Lattanzio, or CRS Report R40506, *Cars, Trucks, and Climate: EPA Regulation of Greenhouse Gases from Mobile Sources*.

[6] http://www.epa.gov/otaq/climate/regs-light-duty htm#new1.

[7] U.S. Environmental Protection Agency, U.S. Department of Transportation, "Greenhouse Gas Emissions Standards and Fuel Efficiency Standards for Medium- and Heavy-Duty Engines and Vehicles; Final Rules," 76 *Federal Register* 57106, September 15, 2011.

The agency first proposed the power plant New Source Performance Standards (NSPS) on April 12, 2012, with the expectation that the standards would be finalized within a year. The Clean Air Act requires that proposed NSPS be finalized within a year of proposal, but the agency received more than 2.5 million public comments—the most ever for a proposed EPA rule—and it delayed promulgation beyond the statutory deadline. Of particular concern were: the proposed setting of a single standard applicable to both coal-fired and natural gas-fired sources; the reliance on carbon capture and sequestration (CCS) technology as the means by which coal-fired plants would comply with the standard; and the cost and technical feasibility of CCS technology. In general, critics complained that given the cost and unproven nature of CCS, the NSPS would effectively prohibit the construction of new coal-fired power plants.

On June 25, 2013, the President gave new impetus to EPA's GHG regulatory efforts. In a major speech and in a more detailed Climate Action Plan released the same day, the President directed EPA to re-propose GHG standards for new power plants by September 20, and finalize them "in a timely fashion after considering all public comments, as appropriate."[8] More importantly, he directed the agency to propose GHG emission standards for existing power plants by June 2014, with promulgation by June 2015. (For information on the President's directive and on issues related to the Power Plant Carbon Rule, see CRS Report R43127, *EPA Standards for Greenhouse Gas Emissions from Power Plants: Many Questions, Some Answers.*)

The adoption of motor vehicle GHG standards also triggered GHG *permit* requirements for new stationary sources of all types. Section 165 of the Clean Air Act requires preconstruction permits and the imposition of best available control technology for new major sources of all pollutants "subject to regulation" under the act. When the GHG standards for motor vehicles took effect in January 2011, GHGs became subject to regulation, according to the agency, triggering Section 165. Thus, GHG permit requirements took effect January 2, 2011.

EPA has focused its initial permitting efforts on the largest emitters, granting smaller sources at least a six-year reprieve. As of September 2013, only 110 GHG permits had been issued by EPA and state permitting authorities;[9] there are as many as 6 million stationary sources of GHGs, according to EPA, so the permit requirement has effected a very small number of sources. Nevertheless, this triggering of standards for the largest new stationary sources (power plants, manufacturing facilities, and others) has raised substantial concern in Congress and among potentially affected industries.

Legislation introduced in the 112th Congress aimed to prevent EPA from implementing GHG emission requirements. More than a dozen bills were introduced, as well as amendments and riders on appropriations bills. The House passed three of these bills, but the Senate did not follow suit. (For additional detail, see CRS Report R41563, *Clean Air Issues in the 112th Congress.*) Given the President's renewed focus on climate change and continued opposition by many in Congress, legislation to restrict EPA's authority with respect to GHG emissions is considered likely to be considered again in the 113th Congress.

---

[8] Office of the Press Secretary, The White House, "Power Sector Carbon Pollution Standards," Memorandum for the Administrator of the Environmental Protection Agency, June 25, 2013, at http://www.whitehouse.gov/the-press-office/2013/06/25/presidential-memorandum-power-sector-carbon-pollution-standards. See also 78 *Federal Register* 39535, July 1, 2013.

[9] Personal communication, U.S. EPA Office of Air Quality Planning and Standards, September 18, 2013.

EPA's GHG regulations have also been challenged in court. On June 26, 2012, the D.C. Circuit Court of Appeals dismissed challenges to four agency regulations: the GHG endangerment finding, emission standards for light duty vehicles, and two rules related to the permitting of GHG emissions from large stationary sources.[10] On October 15, 2013, the Supreme Court agreed to review one aspect of the D.C. Circuit ruling: "[w]hether EPA permissibly determined that its regulation of greenhouse gas emissions from new motor vehicles triggered permitting requirements under the Clean Air Act for stationary sources that emit greenhouse gases." The case, now styled *Utility Air Regulatory Group v. EPA*, likely will be decided by June 2014. (For additional information, see CRS Legal Sidebar WSLG692, *The Supreme Court Agrees to Review EPA's Greenhouse Gas Regulations—Limited to a Narrow Question*, by Robert Meltz.)

Emissions of Other Pollutants from Power Plants

Issues related to emissions other than GHGs from electric power plants—principally sulfur dioxide (SO_2), nitrogen oxides (NOx), and mercury—may be another focus of interest in the 113ᵗʰ Congress. Bush Administration regulations addressing these emissions were vacated by the D.C. Circuit Court of Appeals in two 2008 decisions (*North Carolina v. EPA* and *New Jersey v. EPA*). As a result, EPA has developed new regulations to address the court's concerns. It promulgated regulations addressing SO_2 and NOx on August 8, 2011, and for power plant emissions of mercury and other hazardous air pollutants on February 16, 2012.

Coal-fired power plants are among the largest sources of air pollution in the United States. In 2005, they accounted for 10.2 million tons of sulfur dioxide (SO_2) emissions (70% of the U.S. total), 52 tons of mercury emissions (46% of the U.S. total), and 3.6 million tons of nitrogen oxides (19% of the U.S. total). Power plants are considered major sources of fine particles ($PM_{2.5}$), many of which form in the atmosphere from emissions from a wide range of stationary and mobile sources. In addition, they account for about one-third of U.S. anthropogenic emissions of greenhouse gases, in the form of carbon dioxide.

Under the Clean Air Act, however, power plants have not necessarily been subject to stringent requirements: emissions and the required control equipment can vary depending on the location of the plant, when it was constructed, whether it has undergone major modifications, the specific type of fuel it burns, and, to some extent, the vagaries of state and EPA enforcement policies. More than half a dozen separate Clean Air Act programs could potentially be used to control emissions, which makes compliance strategy complicated for utilities and difficult for regulators. Because the cost of the most stringent available controls, for the entire industry, could range into the tens of billions of dollars, utilities have fought hard and rather successfully to limit or delay regulations affecting them, particularly with respect to plants constructed before the Clean Air Act of 1970 was passed. This group, which includes about one-third of coal-fired capacity, are generally referred to as "grandfathered" plants.

As discussed below under "Air Quality Standards," new ambient air quality standards for ozone, fine particles, and SO_2 will be taking effect in the next few years. Emissions of NOx and SO_2 will have to be reduced further to meet these standards. (NOx contributes to the formation of ozone and fine particles; SO_2, besides being a regulated pollutant in its own right, is among the sources of fine particles.)

---

[10] Coalition for Responsible Regulation, Inc. v. EPA, 684 F.3d 102 (D.C. Cir. 2012).

The continuing controversy over the interpretation of New Source Review requirements for existing power plants (which require the installation of Best Available Control Technology whenever an existing power plant undergoes major modifications) has exerted pressure for a more predictable regulatory structure, as well.

Thus, some in industry, environmental groups, Congress, and the last three Administrations have said that legislation addressing power plant pollution in a comprehensive (multi-pollutant) fashion would be desirable. Such legislation would address the major pollutants on a coordinated schedule and would rely, to a large extent, on a system such as the one used in the acid rain program, where national or regional caps on emissions are implemented through a system of tradable allowances. The key questions were how stringent the caps should be and whether carbon dioxide (CO_2), the major gas of concern with regard to climate change, would be among the emissions subject to a cap. The Senate Environment and Public Works Committee voted twice on a multi-pollutant bill (in 2002 and 2005), but neither of the bills progressed to the Senate floor. In the House, similar bills were introduced, but none progressed to markup.

Cross-State Air Pollution / Clean Air Interstate Rule (CAIR)

Unable to obtain congressional approval of its multi-pollutant bill (the "Clear Skies" bill), the Bush Administration's EPA announced on March 10, 2005, that it would use existing Clean Air Act authority to promulgate final regulations similar to those in the bill for utility emissions of SO_2 and NOx in 27 eastern states and the District of Columbia.[11]

The Clean Air Interstate Rule (CAIR) established cap-and-trade provisions for SO_2 and NOx. A separate regulation, the Clean Air Mercury Rule (CAMR), promulgated at the same time, established a cap-and-trade system for mercury emissions.[12] CAIR covered only the eastern half of the country, but since most of the grandfathered generation capacity is located there (in the East, Midwest, and South), EPA projected that nationwide emissions of SO_2 would decline 53% by 2015 and NOx emissions 56%, as compared to nationwide emissions in 2001. The agency also projected that the rule would result in $85 billion-$100 billion in health benefits annually by 2015, including the annual prevention of 17,000 premature deaths. CAIR's health and environmental benefits would be more than 25 times greater than its costs, according to EPA.[13]

North Carolina v. EPA

CAIR was one of the few Bush Administration environmental initiatives that was generally supported by environmentalists. It also had broad support in the regulated community. But a variety of petitioners, including the state of North Carolina and other downwind states, which argued that the rule was not strong enough to address pollution from upwind sources, and some individual utilities that felt they were unfairly treated by the rule's emission budgets, challenged the rule in the D.C. Circuit, and the court vacated it July 11, 2008. A unanimous court found that

---

[11] The rule appeared in the *Federal Register* two months later. See U.S. EPA, "Ambient air quality standards, national—Fine particulate matter and ozone; interstate transport control measures," 70 *Federal Register* 25162, May 12, 2005.

[12] 70 *Federal Register* 28606, May 18, 2005.

[13] See U.S. EPA, Office of Air and Radiation, *Regulatory Impact Analysis for the Final Clean Air Interstate Rule*, March 2005, pp. 3-3 and 3-4, at http://www.epa.gov/cair/pdfs/finaltech08.pdf.

although EPA had established a "significant contribution" made by power plants to nonattainment of standards and failure to maintain standards in downwind states, as required by Section 110 of the Clean Air Act, the agency's methodology for establishing emission budgets for each state was unrelated to the state's contribution to the nonattainment and maintenance problems in specific downwind states.[14] The court also found that the choice of 2015 for a second phase compliance deadline, based on technological and economic feasibility, ignored EPA's statutory mandate. It found the fuel adjustment factors in the rule (which set more stringent requirements for natural gas- and oil-fired plants than for coal-fired ones) to be arbitrary and capricious. It concluded: "CAIR's flaws are deep. No amount of tinkering ... will transform CAIR, as written, into an acceptable rule."[15] On December 23, 2008, the court modified its decision, however, allowing CAIR to remain in effect until a new rule is promulgated by EPA. [16]

Although they differ on the details of what they support, states, electric utilities, and environmental groups have all supported a replacement that is similar to CAIR in many respects. Without CAIR, most eastern states would have an enormous challenge in achieving ambient air quality standards through in-state emission reductions. For the utilities, CAIR was designed to build on the existing regulatory framework of cap-and-trade programs under the acid rain program and the "NOx SIP Call."[17] Anticipating the ability to bank and trade emission allowances under CAIR, numerous utilities had already installed equipment to meet or exceed CAIR's requirements, the first phase of which have now been implemented. Environmental groups have argued for a stronger version of CAIR—particularly its second phase, to be implemented in 2015—but they generally support the basic approach.

EPA's CAIR Replacement: The Cross-State Air Pollution Rule

On July 6, 2011, EPA finalized a replacement for CAIR, the Cross-State Air Pollution Rule (CSAPR, generally pronounced as "Casper").[18] CSAPR would leave the CAIR Phase 1 limits in place and would have set new limits replacing CAIR's second phase in 2012 and 2014, up to three years earlier than CAIR would have.

The CAIR Phase 1 rules have already had a substantial effect. In 2010, EPA reports, SO_2 emissions from fossil-fueled power plants in the lower 48 states (at 5.1 million tons) were 49% below 2005 levels. NOx emissions from the same sources declined to 2.1 million tons in 2010, 42% less than in 2005.[19]

CSAPR would build on these reductions. It would have established a second and third phase of reductions in 2012 and 2014, with particular emphasis on SO_2—emissions of which would

---

[14] North Carolina v. EPA, 531 F.3d 896 (D.C. Cir. 2008).

[15] Ibid. at 930.

[16] North Carolina v. EPA, 550 F.3d 1176 (D.C. Cir. 2008).

[17] The acid rain program, established by the Clean Air Act Amendments of 1990, set up a cap-and-trade program for sulfur dioxide emissions from electric generating units. Implementation began in 1995. The NOx SIP Call, implemented in 2004, is a cap-and-trade program for control of nitrogen oxide emissions in the eastern half of the country.

[18] The rule appeared in the *Federal Register*, August 8, 2011. For more details, including a link to the *Federal Register* notice, see http://www.epa.gov/crossstaterule/actions.html.

[19] Data are from EPA's National Emissions Inventory, at http://www.epa.gov/ttn/chief/trends/.

decline to 2.4 million tons in the covered states (73% below 2005 levels) in 2014. The rule would cover 28 Eastern, Midwestern, and Southern states and the District of Columbia.

CSAPR is a modified cap-and-trade rule. It would set emission caps in each of the covered states and allow unlimited trading of allowances within the individual states. Interstate trading would be allowed so long as a state remains within 18%-21% of its emissions caps. Limiting interstate trading was intended to address the D.C. Circuit's *North Carolina* ruling, which found CAIR's unlimited interstate allowance trading program unlawful.

To hasten implementation of CSAPR, EPA promulgated a Federal Implementation Plan (FIP) for each of the states: the FIPs specified emission budgets for each state based on controlling emissions from electric power plants. States may develop their own State Implementation Plans and may choose to control other types of sources if they wish, but the federal plan was to take effect until the state acted to replace it.

EPA estimated that CSAPR would cost the power sector $800 million annually in 2014 (on top of $1.6 billion already being spent to comply with CAIR), but it expects the benefits of the combined spending to be 50 to 120 times as great—an estimated $120 billion to $280 billion annually. The most important benefit would be 13,000 to 34,000 fewer premature deaths annually. Avoided deaths and other benefits occur throughout the East, Midwest, and South, according to EPA, with Ohio and Pennsylvania benefitting the most.[20]

Criticism of the Cross-State rule initially focused on the short time frame for implementation, and the adequacy of the emission "budgets" for some of the covered states. Questions regarding the adequacy of the compliance time frame focused on Phase 1 of the rule, which was to take effect in 2012, just five months after the rule's promulgation. EPA maintained that the deadline was reasonable because no new equipment needed to be installed to meet the 2012 requirements. Compliance could be achieved, according to the agency, by running existing pollution control equipment more frequently or increasing power generation at cleaner generation units. (In fact, preliminary estimates for 2012 show that—despite CSAPR being stayed, as discussed below— emissions of SO_2 and NOx declined by 36% and 19%, respectively, in 2012, largely as a result of utilities switching to natural gas generation.)[21]

A second issue concerned the adequacy of the emissions budgets for individual states. Particular controversy centered on Texas, which was included in the final rule, but not in the proposed version. Following promulgation, EPA reviewed additional information submitted by Texas and revised the rule to increase the state's SO_2 emissions cap by 29%; but the state remained opposed to the rule.

Legislative and Judicial Options

In the 112th Congress, both the House and Senate considered legislation that would have revoked the CSAPR rule. The House bill (H.R. 2401) passed 249-169, on September 23, 2011. The same provisions were included in Title III of H.R. 3409, which the House passed in September 2012.

---

[20] U.S. EPA, Office of Air and Radiation, "Final Air Pollution Cross-State Air Pollution Rule," Overview Presentation, undated, pp. 12-14, at http://www.epa.gov/crossstaterule/pdfs/CSAPRPresentation.pdf.

[21] U.S. EPA, Clean Air Markets Division, "Emissions Tracking Highlights," at http://www.epa.gov/airmarkets/quarterlytracking.html.

The Senate did not take up either House bill, but it did consider S.J.Res. 27, a resolution of disapproval of CSAPR under the Congressional Review Act (CRA). It was rejected by the Senate, 41-56, on November 10, 2011. (For additional detail, see CRS Report R41563, *Clean Air Issues in the 112th Congress*.)

Although unsuccessful in Congress, opponents of the CSAPR rule did prevail in court. At least 45 parties filed suit asking the D.C Circuit Court of Appeals to review the rule (the cases were consolidated as *EME Homer City Generation L.P. v. EPA*). On August 21, 2012, in a 2-1 decision, the court vacated and remanded the rule, finding that EPA's imposition of Federal Implementation Plans, without first giving the states an opportunity to develop their own plans, was unlawful. The court also held that EPA's emission budgets (which were based on what the agency considered cost-effective controls) may require states to reduce their emissions by amounts greater than their significant contribution to nonattainment in downwind states.[22] The agency subsequently petitioned the court for rehearing *en banc*, but the court denied the petition, January 24, 2013. EPA subsequently appealed the D.C. Circuit decision to the Supreme Court, which has agreed to hear the case. Oral argument is scheduled for December 10.

Mercury and Air Toxics Standards

Background

The Clean Air Act also provides authority for EPA to regulate emissions of mercury and other hazardous air pollutants (HAPs, or "air toxics") from electric generation units. Much of this discussion has focused on mercury. Electric generating units account for about half of all mercury emissions in the United States.

Mercury is a persistent, bioaccumulative neurotoxin that can cause adverse health effects (principally delayed development, neurological defects, and lower IQ in fetuses and children) at very low concentrations. (For a discussion of mercury's health effects, see CRS Report RL32420, *Mercury in the Environment: Sources and Health Risks*.) The principal route of exposure to mercury is through consumption of fish. Mercury enters water bodies, often through air emissions, and is taken up through the food chain, ultimately affecting humans as a result of fish consumption. All 50 states have issued fish consumption advisories due to mercury pollution, covering 16.4 million acres of lakes, 1.1 million river miles, and the coastal waters of 16 entire states.[23]

EPA was required by the 1990 Clean Air Act Amendments and a 1998 consent agreement to determine whether regulation of mercury from power plants under Section 112 of the Clean Air Act was appropriate and necessary. Section 112 is the section that regulates emissions of hazardous air pollutants. In general, it requires EPA to set standards based on the Maximum Achievable Control Technology (a term defined with great precision in the act), and to impose the MACT standards at each individual emissions source. In a December 2000 regulatory finding, EPA concluded that regulation of mercury from power plants under Section 112 was appropriate and necessary.

---

[22] EME Homer City Generation, L.P. v. EPA, 696 F.3d 7 (D.C. Cir. 2012).

[23] U.S. EPA, "National Listing of Fish Advisories: Technical Fact Sheet 2010," at http://water.epa.gov/scitech/swguidance/fishshellfish/fishadvisories/technical_factsheet_2010.cfm.

Rather than promulgate MACT standards, however, EPA reversed its December 2000 finding in March 2005, and established through regulations a national cap-and-trade system for power plant emissions of mercury, the Clean Air Mercury Rule (CAMR). Under CAMR, the final cap would have been 15 tons of emissions nationwide in 2018 (about a 70% reduction from 1999 levels, when achieved).

Under the cap-and-trade system, utilities could either control the pollutant directly or purchase excess allowances from other plants that instituted controls more stringently or sooner than required. As with the acid rain and CAIR cap-and-trade programs, early reductions under CAMR could have been banked for later use, which the agency itself (in the Regulatory Impact Analysis of the rule) said would result in utilities delaying compliance with the full 70% reduction until after 2025.[24] (For additional information on the mercury rule, see archived CRS Report RL32868, *Mercury Emissions from Electric Power Plants: An Analysis of EPA's Cap-and-Trade Regulations*.)

New Jersey v. EPA

The CAMR rule was challenged in petitions for review filed by New Jersey and 16 other states as well as other petitioners.[25] The D.C. Circuit, in a 3-0 decision handed down February 8, 2008 (*New Jersey v. EPA*), vacated the rule.[26] The court found that once the agency had listed electric generating units (EGUs) as a source of hazardous air pollutants, it had to proceed with MACT regulations under Section 112 of the act unless it "delisted" the source category, under procedures the act sets forth in Section 112(c)(9). The procedures would require the agency to find that no EGU's emissions exceeded a level adequate to protect public health with an ample margin of safety, and that no adverse environmental effect would result from any source—a difficult test to meet, given the agency's estimate that EGUs were responsible for 46% of mercury emissions from all U.S. sources at the time. Rather than delist the EGU source category, the agency had maintained that it could simply reverse its December 2000 "appropriate and necessary" finding, a decision that was much simpler because there were no statutory criteria to meet. The court found this approach unlawful. "This explanation deploys the logic of the Queen of Hearts, substituting EPA's desires for the plain text of Section 112(c)(9)," the court said in its opinion.[27]

Other Mercury / Air Toxics Issues

Besides the question of whether EPA complied with the law's requirements, critics found other reasons to oppose EPA's cap-and-trade approach to controlling mercury. One of the main criticisms has been that it would not address "hot spots," areas where mercury emissions and/or concentrations in water bodies are greater than elsewhere. In fact, under a cap-and-trade system, nothing would prevent emissions from increasing at hot spots.

Many also argued that the mercury regulations should have been more stringent or implemented more quickly than the cap-and-trade regulations would have required. These arguments found a

---

[24] U.S. EPA, *Regulatory Impact Analysis of the Final Clean Air Mercury Rule*, Table 7-3, p. 7-5, at http://www.epa.gov/ttnecas1/regdata/RIAs/mercury_ria_final.pdf.

[25] Seven other states joined EPA in defending the rule.

[26] New Jersey v. EPA, 517 F.3d 574 (D.C. Cir. 2008).

[27] Id. at 582.

receptive audience in the states: about 20 states have promulgated requirements stricter than the federal Clean Air Mercury Rule program, with several requiring 80% to 90% mercury reductions before 2010. (For additional information, see archived CRS Report RL33535, *Mercury Emissions from Electric Power Plants: States Are Setting Stricter Limits*.)

CAMR also didn't address emissions of hazardous air pollutants other than mercury. According to EPA, EGUs are sources of 12 other HAPs, including three acid gases and nine toxic metals.[28]

The Utility MACT / Mercury and Air Toxics Standards

On February 16, 2012, EPA responded to the *New Jersey v. EPA* court decision by promulgating what is referred to as the "Utility MACT" or the Mercury and Air Toxics Standards (MATS).[29] The standards have been widely debated: between proposal and promulgation, the agency is reported to have received 960,000 public comments on them.

MATS requires coal-fired power plants to achieve a 91% reduction from uncontrolled emissions of mercury, nine other toxic metals, and three acid gases, all of which were listed by Congress as hazardous air pollutants in the 1990 Clean Air Act Amendments. According to EPA, power plants are the largest emitters of many of these pollutants, accounting for about 50% of the nation's mercury emissions, 62% of its arsenic emissions, and 82% of its hydrochloric acid emissions, for example.[30] The MATS rule is also projected to reduce emissions of fine particulates ($PM_{2.5}$); although $PM_{2.5}$ is not listed as a hazardous air pollutant, EPA believes that the MATS rule's effect on $PM_{2.5}$ will lead to the avoidance of up to 11,000 premature deaths each year.

In proposing the standards, EPA noted that while the requirements are stringent for those facilities lacking controls, 56% of existing coal-fired power plants already were equipped with controls that would allow them to meet the standards. Thus, the standards are expected to level the playing field, bringing older, poorly controlled plants up to the standards capable of being achieved by a majority of the existing units. In this respect, the proposed standards reflect the statute's requirement that existing sources of HAPs should meet standards based on the current emissions of the best performing similar sources.

The agency also concludes that some plants would be retired by 2015, rather than invest in control technologies. In all, it says, coal-fired generation would decline about 2% as a result of the MATS rule. Coal-fired capacity is, of course, simultaneously being buffeted by market forces, principally the low cost of natural gas. As a result, more than that 2% of coal-fired generation is being retired. (For additional discussion, see CRS Report R42144, *EPA's Utility MACT: Will the Lights Go Out?*)

---

[28] See U.S. EPA, "Memorandum: Emissions Overview: Hazardous Air Pollutants in Support of the Final Mercury and Air Toxics Standard," November 2011, Tables 4, 5, and 6, at http://www.epa.gov/airquality/powerplanttoxics/pdfs/20111216EmissionsOverviewMemo.pdf. Hereinafter, "EPA Emissions Overview."

[29] The rule appeared in the *Federal Register*, February 16, 2012, at 77 *Federal Register* 9304. For a link to the rule as well as explanatory material, see U.S. EPA, "Final Mercury and Air Toxics Standards (MATS) for Power Plants," at http://www.epa.gov/airquality/powerplanttoxics/actions html.

[30] EPA Emissions Overview, previously cited.

In its Regulatory Impact Analysis,[31] EPA projected the annual cost of compliance with the MATS rule at $9.6 billion. The average consumer would see an increase of $3-$4 per month in the cost of electricity due to the rule, according to the agency. These costs will go largely to the installation of scrubbers and fabric filters. In most cases, the fabric filters will be coupled with activated carbon injection or dry sorbent injection. Mercury and other HAPs become attached to the carbon or sorbent after it is injected into the flue gas, and the fabric filter collects the particles, removing them from the plant's emissions.

This is not complicated or new technology. Other types of facilities (notably solid waste incinerators) have used this technology for the past 15 years to reduce their mercury emissions by 95% or more. Moreover, as a result of state-level pollution control regulations, a growing percentage of coal-fired plants do the same. EPA estimates that about one-fifth of U.S. coal-fired electric generating capacity would have either activated carbon or dry sorbent injection in 2015 without the rule.

The benefits of the rule are estimated by EPA at $37 billion to $90 billion annually—4 to 9 times as great as the costs—due primarily to the avoidance of 4,200 to 11,000 premature deaths each year. Other benefits, only some of which were given dollar values, include the annual avoidance of 4,700 nonfatal heart attacks, 130,000 asthma attacks, and developmental effects on children, including effects on IQ, learning, and memory.

Legislative and Judicial Action

Like the CSAPR rule, the MATS rule has been challenged both in Congress and in the courts. In the 112th Congress, H.R. 2401 and H.R. 3409 would have declared the MATS rule "of no force and effect," would have required that any replacement rule impose the least burdensome regulatory alternative among those authorized under the Clean Air Act, and would have delayed compliance with any replacement rule until six years after an interagency panel completed a study of the cumulative impact of numerous listed EPA rules. The Senate did not consider either bill, but it did consider S.J.Res. 37, a resolution to disapprove the MATS rule under the Congressional Review Act. The resolution was rejected by the Senate, 46-53, on June 20, 2012.

The regulations have also been challenged in the D.C. Circuit Court of Appeals (*White Stallion Energy Center v. EPA*). Oral argument is scheduled for December 10. Petitioners have focused on EPA's "appropriate and necessary" finding, arguing that the agency found few direct benefits from controlling mercury or other air toxics. The vast majority of the monetized benefits in EPA's analysis come from reduced emissions of $PM_{2.5}$, which the pollution control equipment would achieve as a co-benefit.

In the meantime, in response to petitions by numerous parties, EPA agreed to reconsider portions of the MATS rule.[32] On March 28, 2013, the agency modified the rule's standards for mercury

---

[31] U.S. EPA, *Regulatory Impact Analysis for the Final Mercury and Air Toxics Standards*, at http://www.epa.gov/ttn/ecas/regdata/RIAs/matsriafinal.pdf.

[32] U.S. EPA, "Reconsideration of Certain New Source Issues: National Emission Standards for Hazardous Air Pollutants from Coal- and Oil-Fired Electric Utility Steam Generating Units and Standards of Performance for Fossil-Fuel-Fired Electric Utility, Industrial-Commercial-Institutional, and Small Industrial-Commercial-Institutional Steam Generating Units," Final Rule, March 28, 2013. The final rule appeared in the *Federal Register* on April 24, 2013, at 78 *Federal Register* 24073.

emissions from new coal-fired power plants: the modifications will allow 15 times as much mercury to be emitted as would have been allowed under the final standard promulgated in February 2012. The change responded to comments from the Institute of Clean Air Companies (the trade association that manufactures pollution control and monitoring equipment) and others that the mercury standard as originally promulgated was an order of magnitude below a level that could be measured by continuous monitoring equipment.

The reconsideration also makes the new source standards for particulate matter and hydrogen chloride less stringent, allowing 13 times as much particulate matter and 25 times as much hydrogen chloride; these changes were based on the agency's conclusion that it had not used all the available emissions information in the record when it promulgated the February 2012 standards. The agency says that the changes will result in "no significant change in costs, emission reductions or health benefits from MATS." Facilities will still need the same pollution control equipment to meet the less stringent standards.[33]

Cumulative Impacts of EPA Rules

As EPA has developed and proposed standards for electric generating units, utilities that rely heavily on coal-fired power and the industry's trade association, the Edison Electric Institute (EEI), have raised concerns about the cumulative impacts of EPA rules. Besides the CSAPR and MATS rules, their attention has focused on proposed Clean Water Act rules for cooling water intake structures, proposed Solid Waste Disposal Act standards for managing coal combustion wastes, and potential Clean Air Act standards for emissions of greenhouse gases. Cumulatively, many in the industry and other opponents of these regulations have referred to these rules as an impending "train wreck" for coal-fired power plants. They maintain that compliance will be difficult and costly within the mandated timeframes, and that, as a result, sections of the country depending on coal-fired power could experience electricity reliability problems as plants are retired or taken off-line for retrofit of pollution controls.

Others in the industry and in various think tanks have concluded that this is unlikely to be the case. They note that the studies sponsored by EEI and by coal-reliant utilities were generally written before EPA proposed or promulgated any of the actual regulations, and the studies often assumed far more stringent requirements than EPA actually proposed or promulgated. While it is true that many coal-fired units would have to be taken out of service for pollution control equipment to be installed, the next few years would be an opportune time to do so, as there is currently substantial excess generating capacity in the electric power industry in most regions. This reserve margin will continue to be available over the next 5-10 years: as a result of the recession and the slow pace of economic recovery, demand for electricity is growing slowly.

Many observers note, too, that EPA regulation is only one element of the situation facing aging coal-fired power plants, many of which are more than 40 years old and have few pollution controls. Equally important is competition from more efficient natural gas combined cycle units, which have taken over a larger share of the electric power market as the price of natural gas has declined. Over the last two decades, more than 80% of new generating capacity has come from these gas-fired units, which are relatively cheap to build and are cleaner and more efficient to

---

[33] U.S. EPA, "Fact Sheet, Updates of the Limits for New Power Plants Under the Mercury and Air Toxics Standards (MATS)," at http://www.epa.gov/mats/pdfs/20130328fs.pdf.

operate than many coal-fired units. Observing the inroads being made by gas-fired generation, many industry observers conclude that portions of the electric power industry are simply experiencing a transition to more efficient power generation sources. (For additional information on this subject, see CRS Report R41914, *EPA's Regulation of Coal-Fired Power: Is a "Train Wreck" Coming?*, and CRS Report R42144, *EPA's Utility MACT: Will the Lights Go Out?*)

If the cost of making a coal-fired plant more efficient and less polluting is higher than that of converting to natural gas, the plant may well be retired. This can cause economic dislocation in specific communities, but it might not cause a substantial increase in the price of electricity or threaten the reliability of electricity supply. In 2012, for example, as coal-fired generation declined from 42% to 37% of total electric power, the price of electricity declined by 0.3%.[34]

In the 112th Congress, legislation to address the cumulative impacts issue was introduced in both the House and Senate. H.R. 2401, the Transparency in Regulatory Analysis of Impacts on the Nation (TRAIN) Act of 2011, which the House passed September 23, 2011, would have:

- established a panel of representatives from 11 federal agencies to report to Congress by August 2012 on the cumulative economic impact of a number of listed EPA rules, guidelines, and actions concerning clean air and waste management;

- rendered both the Cross-State rule and the MATS rule "of no force and effect";

- reinstated the CAIR rule to replace the Cross-State rule for at least six years following enactment;

- required that any subsequent replacement allow trading of emission allowances among entities irrespective of the states in which they are located;

- delayed promulgation of a replacement for the MATS rule until at least one year after submission of the cumulative impacts report and delayed compliance for at least five years after that date;

- required that the MATS replacement impose the least burdensome regulatory alternative from among the alternatives authorized under the Clean Air Act; and

- required EPA to take into consideration feasibility and cost in setting health-based ambient air quality standards.

The same provisions passed the House a second time as Title III of H.R. 3409, the Stop the War on Coal Act, September 19, 2012. The Senate did not take action on either bill.

Tier 3 Vehicle and Gasoline Standards

In February 2011, EPA began to scope out new emissions standards for conventional pollutants (i.e., non-greenhouse gases) from passenger cars and light trucks, pursuant to a May 2010 memorandum from the White House that directed the agency to review the adequacy of the current "Tier 2" emissions standards for these vehicles. The Tier 2 standards were finalized in February 2000, and they were phased in between Model Years 2004 and 2009. Having

---

[34] U.S. Energy Information Administration, *Electric Power Monthly*, January 2013, Table ES1.B.

determined that further emission reductions from motor vehicles are essential to attainment of ambient air quality standards in numerous areas, EPA announced proposed Tier 3 standards March 29, 2013. The standards were formally proposed in the *Federal Register* on May 21.[35]

As with the Tier 2 standards, the proposed Tier 3 standards include changes to both vehicle emission limits and fuel formulation rules, lowering the allowable sulfur content of gasoline. Removing sulfur from gasoline improves the performance of existing emission controls and facilitates the use of new technology. The proposal would lower allowable sulfur from 30 parts per million (ppm) to a maximum of 10 ppm, and would require reductions in light duty vehicle emissions of 70%-80%. Requirements would be phased in between 2017 and 2025. In addition to the light duty vehicle emission and gasoline standards, the proposal also extends the required useful life of emission control equipment from 120,000 miles to 150,000 miles, and sets standards for heavier duty gasoline-powered vehicles.

In letters to the President before the standards' proposal, several Senators of both parties asked that the Administration delay the EPA rulemaking over concerns that the new fuel standards would raise the price of gasoline;[36] but EPA maintains that the rule as proposed would add less than a penny to the price of a gallon, while reducing emissions by an amount equivalent to removing 33 million cars from the road. These numbers are disputed by petroleum refiners, but other stakeholders, including the auto industry, are generally in support. Auto manufacturers already face more stringent requirements in California, and fear having to meet a patchwork of standards in different states. They also note that lower sulfur fuel is needed to support the lean-burn technologies that they will use to meet already promulgated fuel efficiency and GHG standards.[37]

The EPA proposal is also supported by environment and public health groups, and by a number of governors and other state and local officials, because it will help nonattainment areas comply with ambient air quality standards. Without tighter standards on vehicles and gasoline, ozone nonattainment areas in most Northeastern states would have to impose more controls on local sources of ozone precursors and particulates.

As stated, refiners are opposed to the rule: they argue that some refineries will find it more difficult than others to reduce sulfur to the 10 ppm standard, and could face cost increases of as much as nine cents a gallon. To address these concerns, EPA's proposal would allow a three-year delay in compliance for small refiners. It also includes averaging, banking, and trading programs that would give the refining industry flexibility in meeting the standards.

A public comment period on the proposal ran through July 1; public hearings were held in Philadelphia on April 24 and Chicago on April 29. EPA had originally stated its intention to promulgate final standards by the end of 2013. That date has now slipped to February 2014.

---

[35] Links to the proposed standards and related materials are on EPA's website at http://www.epa.gov/otaq/tier3 htm.

[36] See http://www.heitkamp.senate.gov/record.cfm?id=341129, and http://www.epw.senate.gov/public/index.cfm?FuseAction=Minority.PressReleases&ContentRecord_id=a70c480c-ce1b-5ee7-430b-ae4f2e5230d9.

[37] For views of the Auto Alliance, see their testimony at the EPA Tier 3 hearing, at http://www.autoalliance.org/index.cfm?objectid=631E0230-AC48-11E2-9CE9000C296BA163.

Air Quality Standards

The Obama Administration's EPA has also reviewed several national ambient air quality standards (NAAQS), as it is required to do by Section 109 of the Clean Air Act. NAAQS don't directly regulate emissions from sources of pollution; rather, they represent EPA's formal judgment regarding how clean the air must be to protect public health and welfare. The standards set in motion monitoring and planning requirements, which in turn can lead to designation of "nonattainment areas" and the imposition of emission controls.

Background

Air quality has improved substantially since the passage of the Clean Air Act in 1970: annual emissions of the six air pollutants for which EPA has set ambient air quality standards (ozone, particulate matter, sulfur dioxide, carbon monoxide, nitrogen dioxide, and lead) have declined by 202 million tons (68%), despite major increases in population, motor vehicle miles traveled, and economic activity.[38] Nevertheless, the goal of clean air continues to elude many areas, in part because scientific understanding of the health effects of air pollution has caused EPA to tighten standards for most of these pollutants. Congress anticipated that the understanding of air pollution's effects on public health and welfare would change with time, and it required, in Section 109(d) of the act, that EPA review the standards at five-year intervals and revise them, as appropriate.

The most widespread problems involve ozone and fine particles. A recent study by researchers at the Massachusetts Institute of Technology concluded, for example, that emissions of particulate matter and ozone caused 210,000 premature deaths in the United States in 2005.[39] Many other studies have found links between air pollution, illness, and premature mortality, as well. EPA summarizes these studies in what are called Integrated Science Assessments and Risk Analyses when it reviews the NAAQS, and it identifies areas where concentrations of pollution exceed the NAAQS following its promulgation. As of July 2013, 123 million people lived in areas classified "nonattainment" for the ozone NAAQS; 73 million lived in areas that were nonattainment for the fine particle ($PM_{2.5}$) NAAQS.[40]

Violations of the ambient air quality standards for the other four criteria pollutants are not as widespread, but EPA is engaged in (or has recently completed) reviews indicating that health effects of most of these pollutants are more serious and more prevalent than previously thought. As recently as 2010, for example, no areas exceeded the NAAQS for sulfur dioxide (SO_2), but in a review concluded in that year, EPA determined that between 2,300 and 5,900 premature deaths could be avoided annually by strengthening that standard.[41] The agency now concludes that 1.2

---

[38] For additional data on air pollution trends, see http://www.epa.gov/airtrends/aqtrends html#comparison.

[39] Fabio Caiazzo, et al., "Air Pollution and Early Deaths in the United States. Part I: Quantifying the Impact of Major Sectors in 2005," *Atmospheric Environment*, November 2013, pp. 198-208.

[40] Data for ozone nonattainment areas are from the U.S. EPA "Green Book," at http://www.epa.gov/airquality/greenbk/ hntc html. Data for $PM_{2.5}$ nonattainment areas are also from the "Green Book," at http://www.epa.gov/airquality/ greenbk/rntc html.

[41] U.S. EPA, "Revisions to the Primary National Ambient Air Quality Standard, Monitoring Network and Data Reporting Requirements for Sulfur Dioxide (SO_2)," Text Slides, June 2010, p. 21, at http://www.epa.gov/air/ sulfurdioxide/pdfs/20100603presentation.pdf.

million people live in areas that are nonattainment for a revised SO$_2$ NAAQS. A review of the lead standard completed in 2008 concluded that it should be lowered by 90%,[42] as a result of which nearly 10 million people are considered to live in areas with unhealthy levels of atmospheric lead.[43]

CRS Report R41563, *Clean Air Issues in the 112th Congress*, summarized EPA's recent efforts to review the NAAQS and implement revisions, including the next steps for each of the six criteria pollutants. Reviews of all six pollutants (ozone, PM, lead, NO$_2$, carbon monoxide, and SO$_2$) have been completed since 2006, with the standards being made more stringent for five of the six. The next round of reviews has begun for ozone and lead.

Reviews don't always lead to revision of the standards. On August 31, 2011, the EPA Administrator completed a review of the carbon monoxide (CO) NAAQS without changing the standard. The CO standard was promulgated in its present form in 1971.

Ozone and PM NAAQS Reviews

Since 2010, two NAAQS reviews, for ozone and for PM, have proven particularly controversial. The next sections provide a brief discussion of the two reviews.

Ozone

On January 19, 2010, EPA proposed a revision to the NAAQS for ozone.[44] The proposal did not follow the usual five-year (or longer) review process, but resulted from the EPA Administrator's decision to reconsider standards promulgated in March 2008 by the previous Administration. The 2008 review had made the standards more stringent; but EPA suspended implementation of the new standard in September 2009 in order to consider further strengthening it, and proposed a more stringent standard in January 2010.

As proposed, the January 2010 revision would have lowered the primary (health-based) standard from 75 parts per billion (ppb) averaged over 8 hours (the standard set in 2008) to somewhere in the range of 70 to 60 ppb; it would also have set a new secondary standard designed to protect crops and forests from ozone. The proposal followed the recommendations of the agency's panel of outside scientific advisers, the Clean Air Scientific Advisory Committee (CASAC), which had concluded that the 2008 revision did not meet the Clean Air Act's statutory requirements.

Because of its wide reach and potential cost, the proposed revision was among the most controversial rules under consideration at EPA at the time. EPA is prohibited by the statute from considering costs in setting NAAQS,[45] but it does prepare cost and benefit estimates for

---

[42] U.S. EPA, "Fact Sheet, Final Revisions to the National Ambient Air Quality Standards for Lead," 2008, at http://www.epa.gov/air/sulfurdioxide/pdfs/20100603presentation.pdf.

[43] U.S. EPA, Green Book, at http://www.epa.gov/oaqps001/greenbk/popexp html.

[44] U.S. Environmental Protection Agency, "National Ambient Air Quality Standards for Ozone; Proposed Rule," 75 *Federal Register* 2938, January 19, 2010.

[45] The Clean Air Act's §108 and §109 have been so interpreted since the NAAQS provisions were added to the act in 1970; in 2001, this interpretation was affirmed in a unanimous Supreme Court decision, *Whitman v. American Trucking Associations*, 531 U.S. 457 (2001). This is not to say that cost considerations play no role in Clean Air Act decisions: cost-effectiveness is considered extensively by EPA and the states in selecting emission control options. But in (continued...)

---

information purposes, and in order to comply with Executive Order 12866 (under which the Office and Management and Budget (OMB) requires cost-benefit analysis of economically significant rules). When it proposed the 2010 revisions, the agency estimated that the costs of implementing the revised ozone NAAQS would range from $19 billion to $25 billion annually in 2020 if the standard chosen were 70 ppb, or $52 billion to $90 billion if the standard chosen were 60 ppb, with benefits of roughly the same amount.[46] EPA identified at least 515 counties that would violate the NAAQS if the most recent three years of data available at the time of proposal were used to determine attainment (compared to 85 counties that violated the 1997 standard in effect at that time).

Initially, the agency said it would complete the ozone review by August 2010, but it announced delays in the projected completion date four times, before sending a final decision to OMB for interagency review in July 2011. The agency's final decision would have set a 70 ppb primary standard and would have adopted the new form of the secondary standard[47] that the agency had proposed. The agency's cost estimate was unchanged from the proposal—$19 billion to $25 billion in 2020—and quantifiable benefits were estimated to range from $11 billion to $37 billion.[48]

On September 2, 2011, the White House announced that the President had requested that EPA Administrator Jackson withdraw the all-but-final ozone standards from further consideration at that time. The President's statement noted that "work is already underway to update a 2006 review of the science that will result in the reconsideration of the ozone standard in 2013," and stated that he did not "support asking state and local governments to begin implementing a new standard that will soon be reconsidered."[49]

State and local governments *are* being asked to begin implementing a new standard that will soon be reconsidered, however: withdrawal of the decision left EPA and state and local governments to implement the 2008 ozone standards, which had been stayed pending the agency's reconsideration. Following the withdrawal, EPA proceeded with implementation of the 2008 standards, designating nonattainment areas in May and June of 2012. The vast majority of areas

---

(...continued)

deciding what level of ambient pollution poses a health threat, the statute bars consideration of costs.

[46] U.S. EPA, "Fact Sheet: Supplement to the Regulatory Impact Analysis for Ozone," January 7, 2010, at http://www.epa.gov/air/ozonepollution/pdfs/fs20100106ria.pdf.

[47] The Clean Air Act (in Section 109) requires primary standards to protect public health and secondary standards to protect public welfare. Welfare includes effects on soils, water, crops, vegetation, man-made materials, animals, and climate, among other factors. In general, EPA has set both primary and secondary NAAQS at the same level and in the same form. Increasingly, however, the agency's science advisers have concluded that protecting public welfare may require measuring exposures and concentrations over different time periods, using different indicators. For a discussion of how this has affected the secondary standard for ozone, see CRS Report R43092, *Ozone Air Quality Standards: EPA's 2013 Revision.*

[48] The estimated costs compared implementation of a 70 ppb primary standard to a baseline that assumed compliance with the 1997 ozone standard. Implementing the 2008 ozone standard, which the agency is now doing, will cost $7.6 billion to $8.8 billion in 2020 compared to the same baseline, according to the agency; so the incremental cost of the 70 ppb standard would have been on the order of $11 billion to $16 billion. Incremental benefits would also be less if one assumed compliance with the 2008 ozone standard as the baseline. See U.S. EPA, *Regulatory Impact Analysis, Final National Ambient Air Quality Standard for Ozone,* July 2011, p.6, at http://www.epa.gov/airquality/ozonepollution/pdfs/201107_OMBdraft-OzoneRIA.pdf.

[49] The White House, Office of the Press Secretary, "Statement by the President on the Ozone National Ambient Air Quality Standards," September 2, 2011.

---

designated nonattainment for the 2008 standard (**Figure 1**) are areas that had already been designated nonattainment for the previous (1997) standard, but implementation of new, more stringent standards meant that State Implementation Plans and the pollution control measures that they specify could need revision.

Figure 1. Ozone Nonattainment Areas (2008 Standard)

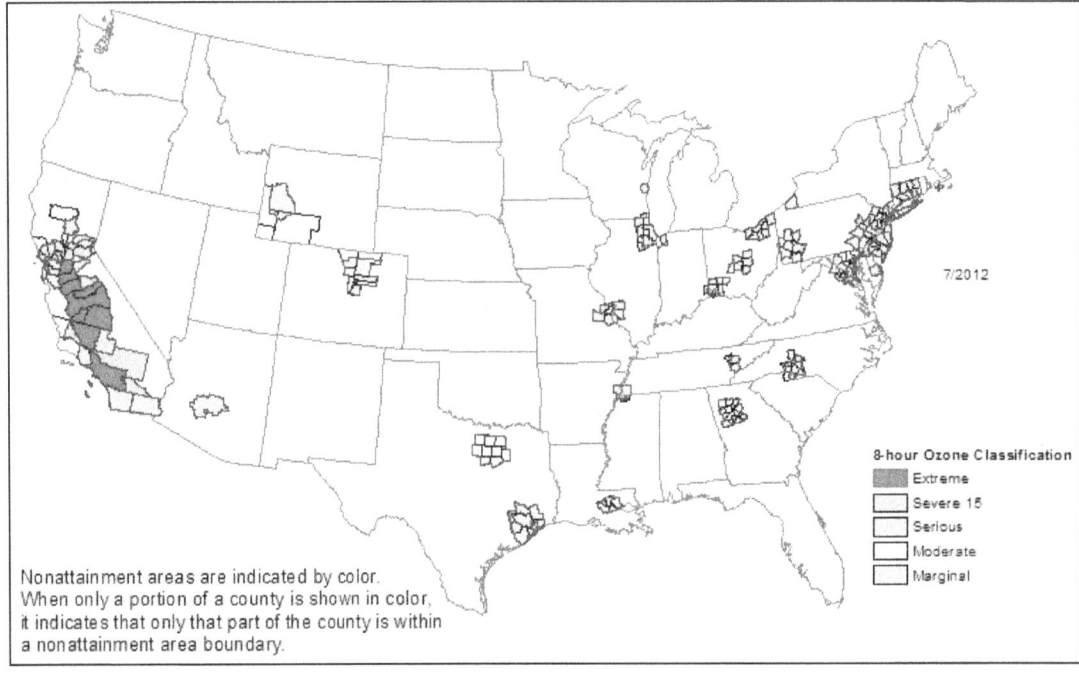

Source: U.S. EPA Green Book.

Meanwhile, EPA has proceeded with the regularly scheduled five-year review of the 2008 standard, as the President indicated the agency would. Proposed revisions as a result of this review are now expected in 2014, with final decisions perhaps a year later. Congress is likely to take a keen interest in the results of this review as it nears completion.

Withdrawing the proposed standards in 2011 also meant that legal challenges to the 2008 standard (*Mississippi v. EPA*), which had been stayed pending the agency's reconsideration, could proceed. The D.C. Circuit decided the case July 23, 2013.[50] In its decision, the court affirmed EPA's 2008 decision as regards the primary ozone NAAQS, but remanded the secondary standard to the agency.

The practical effect of the *Mississipi* decision is unclear, because to a large extent events have passed it by. EPA staff have already completed the Integrated Science Assessment for the next ozone NAAQS review, and the second (potentially final) draft of the staff's recommendations to

---

[50] Mississippi v. EPA, 723 F.3d 246 (D.C. Cir. 2013).

the Administrator as to the form and level of the standards is to be released by March 2014. A decision concerning revision of the ozone standard would likely be proposed in 2014 whether or not the court had remanded the secondary standard.

Particulate Matter (Including "Farm Dust")

The other NAAQS review that was controversial in the 112th Congress—and may continue to be in the 113th—is the review of the particulate matter (PM) standard. EPA considers particulate matter to be among the most serious air pollutants, responsible for tens of thousands of premature deaths annually.

The current NAAQS sets standards for both "fine" particulates ($PM_{2.5}$) and larger, "coarse" particles (PM_{10}). Of the two types of particulates, $PM_{2.5}$ is considered the more significant threat to health; the $PM_{2.5}$ standards also affect far more people and far more counties than the standard for PM_{10}.[51]

EPA completed a review of the PM NAAQS in 2006. The agency is required by the Clean Air Act to review NAAQS at five-year intervals, so another review was due in 2011. As the review process was getting underway, in February 2009, the D.C. Circuit Court of Appeals remanded the 2006 standard for $PM_{2.5}$ to EPA, saying that the standard was "contrary to law and unsupported by adequately reasoned decisionmaking."[52] As a result, EPA combined the statutory five-year review of the standard and its response to the D.C. Circuit decision, completing a review of the PM standard that served both purposes in December 2012.[53] The review left the standard for coarse particles unchanged, as well as the standard for 24-hour exposures to $PM_{2.5}$. But it lowered the standard for annual exposures to $PM_{2.5}$, as suggested by the agency's outside scientific advisers,[54] from 15 micrograms per cubic meter to 12.

Although this appears to be a significant strengthening of a standard that potentially affects a wide array of mobile and stationary sources, EPA projects the incremental cost of the revision at a relatively modest $53 million to $350 million annually. (By way of comparison, as noted earlier, the proposed ozone NAAQS revision in 2010 was projected to cost at least $19 billion per year.) The cost of compliance with the PM NAAQS is moderated by the fact that other EPA standards are reducing exposures to $PM_{2.5}$ even without a strengthening of the ambient standard. Annual benefits were estimated to range from $4.0 billion to $9.1 billion.[55]

The revision also is projected to add relatively few areas to those considered nonattainment for the $PM_{2.5}$ standard. **Figure 2** shows areas currently designated nonattainment for the 15

---

[51] For current data on $PM_{2.5}$ and PM_{10} nonattainment areas and affected populations, see the EPA Green Book at http://www.epa.gov/oaqps001/greenbk/index html.

[52] American Farm Bureau Fed'n v. EPA, 559 F.3d 512 (D.C. Cir. 2009).

[53] The rule appeared in the *Federal Register*, January 15, 2013, at 78 *Federal Register* 3086.

[54] Section 109(d) of the Clean Air Act required the EPA Administrator to appoint an independent scientific review committee, the Clean Air Scientific Advisory Committee (CASAC), which reviews EPA's staff work in setting NAAQS. The Administrator is not required to follow CASAC recommendations, but she must set forth CASAC's findings and, if the NAAQS differs from CASAC recommendations, provide an explanation in the *Federal Register* of the reasons for such differences.

[55] For additional information, see U.S. EPA, "Overview of EPA's Revisions to the Air Quality Standards for Particle Pollution (Particulate Matter)," at http://www.epa.gov/pm/2012/decfsoverview.pdf.

---

microgram standard as well as areas that would exceed the new annual standard if designations were made based on currently available data.

In the 112th Congress, attention to PM issues focused on the larger, coarse particles, PM_{10}, even though EPA did not propose to change them. Members of the House and Senators discussed the need to prevent a supposed EPA plan to use the revision of the PM_{10} standard to impose controls on "farm dust." The House passed legislation to prevent EPA from tightening standards for PM_{10} for one year and to permanently limit EPA's authority to regulate dust in rural areas. EPA stated early in the PM review process that it did not intend to change the PM_{10} standard. The final revision made no change.

(For additional information on the PM standards, see CRS Report R42934, *Air Quality: EPA's 2013 Changes to the Particulate Matter (PM) Standard.*)

Figure 2. Counties Not Meeting the January 2013 Revised Primary Annual PM$_{2.5}$ NAAQS Based on 2009-2011 Air Monitoring Data

(revised annual standard of 12 µg/m³)

Source: Created by CRS using data from the U.S. Environmental Protection Agency (EPA)— http://www.epa.gov/airquality/particlepollution/2012/20092011table.pdf. Base Map: Esri and U.S. Census. Projection: Lambert Conformal Conic. US_Counties_FineParticle_juzel.mxd. February 4, 2013. EPA maps and supporting documents regarding the January 2013 PM$_{2.5}$ NAAQS revisions are available on EPA's website *Particulate Matter (PM): Regulatory Actions*, http://www.epa.gov/pm/actions.html.

Notes: Counties not meeting the January 2013 revised annual standard are presented for illustrative purposes only. EPA will not designate areas as nonattainment for the revised PM$_{2.5}$ NAAQS based on 2009-2011 air monitoring data. Designations will most likely be based on 2011-2013 air monitoring data that the agency anticipates will indicate comparatively improved air quality.

Other Issues

Since 2009, EPA has proposed and promulgated numerous regulations implementing the Clean Air Act (and other pollution control statutes that it administers). Critics of the Administration, both within Congress and outside of it, have accused the agency of reaching beyond the authority given it by Congress and ignoring or underestimating the costs and economic impacts of these rules. At least seven bills that would have overturned specific regulations or limited the agency's authority (H.R. 1, H.R. 910, H.R. 1633, H.R. 2250, H.R. 2401, H.R. 2681, and H.R. 3409) passed the House in the 112th Congress.

In addition to the regulation of greenhouse gas emissions, power plants, and NAAQS, discussed above, two of the EPA regulations that attracted the most attention were the Maximum Achievable Control Technology standards for cement kilns and boilers (referred to as the "Portland Cement MACT," and the "Boiler MACT," respectively). In both cases, EPA agreed to reconsider rules that it had promulgated. On December 20, 2012, EPA Administrator Jackson signed revised rules for both, giving the affected industries additional time to comply, and making the final standards less stringent than those originally promulgated.[56]

While EPA has been widely criticized by industry groups and many in Congress for overreaching, the agency maintains that in promulgating these and other rules, it is complying with statutory mandates placed on the agency by Congress. The agency states that its critics' focus on the cost of controls obscures the benefits of new regulations, which, it estimates, far exceed the costs; and it maintains that pollution control is an important source of economic activity, exports, and American jobs.

Environmental groups generally disagree that the agency has overreached in setting Clean Air Act standards. These groups often maintain that the agency's standards are not stringent enough, don't meet statutory requirements, or disregard the findings of the agency's science advisors. The result is that EPA Clean Air Act standards generally are challenged in court both by industry and by environmental groups, with various states supporting each side. The resulting court decisions often set EPA's agenda as much as Congress or the Administration.

Confirmation of a new EPA Administrator as well as oversight hearings gave the 113th Congress early venues to revisit these issues. A confirmation hearing for Gina McCarthy, President Obama's nominee to lead the agency, was held by the Senate Environment and Public Works Committee on April 11. She was confirmed as EPA Administrator on July 18.

For additional discussion of EPA's regulatory actions, primarily under the Clean Air Act, but also under other statutes, see CRS Report R41561, *EPA Regulations: Too Much, Too Little, or On Track?*

---

[56] The Boiler MACT standards were published January 31, 2013, at 78 *Federal Register* 7138. The Portland Cement rule was published February 12, 2013, at 78 *Federal Register* 10006.

Author Contact Information

James E. McCarthy
Specialist in Environmental Policy
jmccarthy@crs.loc.gov, 7-7225